CONSCIOUSNESS
Source of
CREATION, SPIRITUALITY
&
ETERNAL LIFE

HALIM OZKAPTAN, PH.D.

Copyright © 2015 Oz Associates, LLC
www.booksbyoz.com
hozkaptan@gmail.com

All rights reserved. No part of this book may be reproduced, stored, or transmitted by any means—whether auditory, graphic, mechanical, or electronic—without written permission of both publisher and author, except in the case of brief excerpts used in critical articles and reviews. Unauthorized reproduction of any part of this work is illegal and is punishable by law.

ISBN: 978-0-578-16015-3 (sc)
ISBN: 978-1-4834-2964-9 (e)

Because of the dynamic nature of the Internet, any web addresses or links contained in this book may have changed since publication and may no longer be valid. The views expressed in this work are solely those of the author and do not necessarily reflect the views of the publisher, and the publisher hereby disclaims any responsibility for them.

Any people depicted in stock imagery provided by Thinkstock are models, and such images are being used for illustrative purposes only.
Certain stock imagery © Thinkstock.

Cover Picture: NASA Andromeda Galaxy Picture

Lulu Publishing Services rev. date: 4/16/2015

Other Books by Dr. Halim Ozkaptan
www.booksbyoz.com

Dr. Ozkaptan's books address the dimensions of human life and existence. They answer such important questions as: the purpose of our existence on earth; the meaning and sustainment of true love; the raising of well-adjusted children; the development of and reasons for courage and heroism; the achievement of success through personal resolve; and the source of human spirituality. The similarities of Islam, Christianity and Judaism are also discussed and explained. Through one or more of these books, you will gain insights into the reasons for your own experiences and those of others. They will enrich your understanding of life, and the importance of your personal development and responsibility for the gift of life. They give hope for and explain the eternal spirit which resides within us all.

"Conquering Fear, Development of Courage in Soldiers and Other High Risk Occupations": Addresses the basis of heroism, the willingness to face danger, and how to develop it.

"Life's Purpose, Development of Your Living and Eternal Spirit": Addresses our spiritual nature, its development and why we are on earth.

"Beyond Love, The Fulfillment of Love and Marriage": Discusses the reasons for love and lasting marriage.

"Love is not Enough, to Prepare Your Child for Life's Challenges": Describes the challenging task of how to raise children in today's society.

"Islam and the Koran, Described and Defended": Describes the Koran, Moslem beliefs and their relationship to Christianity and Judaism.

"Overcoming Life's Struggles for Success and Happiness": Addresses the importance of human resolve to face life's inevitable challenges in order to find success and happiness.

"Power of Courage in Combat and Danger": An expanded version of "Conquering Fear", with additional military topics.

Books can be purchased at Amazon, Nook, Kindle, Lulu.com, and www.booksbyoz.com. They are also available as e-publications at Apple ITunes.

Dedication

Dedicated to my: mother Roukia; father Mehmet; wife Elinor; children: William, Peter, Ruthann, and Kenneth; grandchildren: Lauren, Tuula, Erik, Ellen, Kayla and Peter; and to all my friends, past and present, who have enriched my life with their friendship, love and goodwill.

Acknowledgment

My thanks to my wife Elinor, for her many reviews, suggestions and editing.

My thanks also to Adriane Pontecorvo of Lulu Publishing for her gracious and professional production of this book.

CONTENTS

Prologue	xv
1. *Introduction*	*1*
2. *Creation*	*3*
3. *Consciousness*	*7*
Consciousness and the Brain	7
Consciousness the Source of Creation	8
Other Dimensions of Consciousness	10
4. *Your Spiritual Nature*	*13*
Spiritual Source	13
Spiritual Challenge	14
Spiritual Relationships	17
The Soul	18
Evil	19
5. *Manifestations of Your Spiritual Nature and Consciousness*	*21*
Love	21
Faith	21
Goodwill	22
Desire	23
Dreams	23
Hope	23
Prayer	24
Thoughts	25

Beliefs	25
Self-Suggestion	26

6. Life's Purpose — 27
Spiritual Development	27
Self-Realization	29
Loss of Hope and Suicide	31

7. Love and Relationships — 33
Love	33
Marriage	34
Sex	36
Homosexuality	37

8. Why Bad Things Happen — 39
Hardship as a Challenge	40
Hardship as a Deterrent	40
Hardship to Prevent a Greater Loss	41
Hardship as Atonement	42

9. Spiritual Darkness — 45

10. Religion — 49
The Religious Instinct	49
Organized Religion	50
Persons of Faith	52
A Good Person	53

11. Age and Death — 57
Age	57
Death	58

12. The Hereafter — 61
Heaven	61
Hell	62
Reincarnation	63

13. Conclusion — 65

Appendix A: Racial and National Diversity — 67
Racial Diversity 67
National Diversity 68

Appendix B: The Impact of Political Philosophies — 71
Democracy 71
Socialism 72
Communism 73
War 74

References 77

PROLOGUE

At the age of 16, I was a camp counselor in New Jersey. As a resident of New York City, I was overwhelmed by the natural beauty of the YMCA camp. It encompassed over two hundred acres of woods, fields and lakes. I was filled with wonderment about its beauty and harmony with the open and expansive sky. It awakened my spiritual feelings and questions about life's purpose. During that period, when invited to attend church, I would reply that we were already in a cathedral of nature's beauty. This wonderment about nature, its beauty and life's meaning stayed with me, as I grew older and struggled with life's demands for obtaining an education, finding a job, getting married and supporting my family.

When I retired at the age of 70, and after years of contemplation, I wrote a book "Life's Purpose – The Development of Your Living and Eternal Spirit". It was my first attempt to describe our spiritual nature. I later wrote other books attempting to describe and explain the many dimensions of life, such as love, marriage, raising children, self-realization, courage and religion. Despite the specific nature of these subjects, spiritual concepts intruded into many of them. At the age of 85, my spiritual insights coalesced into the present book. It is a much more complete explanation and insight into Life's Purpose.

This book discusses and explains our creation, spiritual reality and purpose in life. It asserts that we are spiritual beings living a mortal life. We are created by and are a part of God's consciousness. Due to our free will, we can make good and bad choices. Our purpose on earth is to test and develop our spiritual and moral worth, in order to become worthy of God's love. In effect, our life on earth is a morality play. On earth we live in a one dimensional system called time. When we pass over after the demise of our body, we remain as part of God's consciousness. At that time, we live in a three dimensional system consisting of the past, present and future. We will review our former life on earth, judge our behavior and feel the pain that we may have caused others. Through reincarnation, we will return to earth to continue our spiritual development and atone for our former sins. When our spiritual development is complete, we will reside in God's presence for eternity.

CHAPTER 1

Introduction

Many people question and wonder how human life and other forms of life on earth occurred. Is there a God, or was life a random event that evolved through natural selection? Is death final or is there reincarnation? Why are we on earth and what is the meaning of life? Are we subject to random and capricious events? These and similar questions challenge the imagination and resist explanation. If there is no God, how can we explain the perfection, interdependence, harmony and beauty of the world? How could the sun cause our food to grow from the soil under our feet? What would explain our vision, hearing, tears, laughter and love? Without a creator or supreme organizing force, the components and interdependence of the world would lack coherence, as well as beauty, and would otherwise be in chaos.

Physicists try to explain our creation from theories such as the Big Bang and subatomic particles. But, these events and physical substances are also the result of creation. It is difficult, or impossible, for the results of creation to explain itself. The question of how and why we were created may only be answerable through our spiritual feelings, insights, and the revelations that come to us. Based on such insights, this book describes how we and the world were created by God's design and consciousness. It describes how our spirituality and soul spring from his consciousness. It explains the reasons for love and evil. It explains that our soul is eternal and that only our body dies. It explains that we are spiritually interconnected with each other. When our present spiritual journey is completed, we pass over and fold back into God's consciousness and love. It talks about the cycle of life through reincarnation, and how we will permanently return to our creator when our spiritual adventure and moral development are completed. We are also bound by linear time, or as Plato said "…the moving image of eternity". We are also "a moment in time and space". When we pass over, we become a part of a three dimensional eternity in what we call heaven, where the past, present and future coexist.

The following sections will discuss how we were created and the relationship between our consciousness, spirituality and soul. How these dimensions are the underpinnings of faith, goodwill and prayer, and what we call coincidences will be explained. The power of thoughts, beliefs, and self-suggestion will be discussed. Life's purpose and the basis for love and happiness will be presented. The reasons for evil and why bad things happen to us will be explained. Heaven and hell will be described. Evaluate and test what is said with your own insights and intuitions. Its validity will become clear as it resonates with your experiences and feelings. Hopefully, the explanations in this book will deepen your spiritual feelings and understanding of why you are on earth.

CHAPTER 2

Creation

Many scientists think that our body, and indeed the world and the life on it, is a miraculous accident. They believe that man emerged from a primal organism that crawled out of the slime and somehow managed and planned its own development into a complex organism, with sight, hearing, taste, emotion, reason and love. Does anyone really believe that the diversity, finely balanced and flawless interdependence and beauty of the world are an accident or a random occurrence? Do they really believe that the air we breathe, the water that we depend upon, and the sun that warms us happened by chance? Have you ever stopped to appreciate the beauty of the world, including its diversity of landscapes, birds, flowers and fish in the sea? Can you imagine a better and more perfect world and creation?

Physicists have postulated several theories to explain the origin of life, such as the Newtonian and Quantum theories. There is also the "Big Bang" theory, whereby the Universe expanded from an extremely dense and hot state, and continues to expand today. Newtonian physicists see the world as perfectly deterministic and predictable. Quantum physicists refer to the indeterminacy of subatomic particles. The physicist, Steven Hawking, even argued that quantum mechanics could explain the origins of life and obviate the need to postulate the existence of God. They assume that they can understand creation from the results of creation that they observe.

Charles Darwin proposed that life evolved through natural selection and evolution, whereby the fittest survived. Some scientists assert that the theory of evolution is proof that God does not exist. Darwin's premise of natural selection, however, does not answer the question of the origin of life. It also cannot explain our feelings of shame, laughter or love. The love between two people, such as a mother's love for her child is proof that God exists. Love derives from his living and eternal spirit that is part of us.

A mother's love for her child is proof that God exits.

Some scientists are beginning to realize that the beginning of life could not have been a random physical event. They cannot explain how our brains function. They have found no way to describe how external stimuli can be transformed by our brain into perception, let alone colors and fragrances. There are also subjective and personal feelings, such as love and remorse, that we experience independent of any external stimulation. These feelings arise inexplicably from a piece of grey matter, our brain. Rene Descartes proposed that the brain and mind must run on different tracks and introduced the concept of dualism, where the mind and brain are connected at the pineal gland.

Think of the wide variety of mammals ranging from man to sheep, horses, cattle and elephants to whales. Our physiology is the same, but did we derive or descend from each other, or a common ancestor? The similarity of physiology in such a large variety of mammals could not have occurred by evolution or chance. Instead, we and they are different species created as if from the "same template of God's design". Think also of the profuse number of different and beautiful flowers, as if purposely designed by a celestial being and artist.

Science cannot explain the origins of life by looking at the "results" of creation or by a material explanation. Our spiritual nature permeates our physical being. The explanation of life's creation can only come from our spiritual insights, experiences, feelings and instincts. The reports of people who have had an out of body experience are another important source. Our faith may also be enough to understand that God is the source of creation. Our ability to think and reason does not contradict our faith. Faith is also rational. It is irrational to believe otherwise.

The world's creation is clearly planned, including our gene structure. It is our gene structure that permits the variation and change of species. Indeed, it is a necessary part of life to enable the continuity, variability and adaptability of human, animal and plant species. A gene structure could not have evolved, but was created to guide evolution and to enable our adaptation to changing environments over the centuries. The capability of genes to evolve is part God's plan. It is easier for many to believe that genes occurred by chance than to believe in a creator. "The doubters come from a sperm drop and deny God's existence".[1]

Why did he[2] create the world? One can only imagine that God wanted to share and expand his spirit, love and creativity. As he imagined us, he created us. His living and eternal spirit exists through us and his creations. His spirit permeates the world and universe and is pervasive. God does not exist as a separate and isolated being, but is an integral part of our reality, consciousness and existence.

> *God is an integral part of our reality, consciousness and existence.*

---

[1] A verse in the Koran.
[2] By use of the word "he", I mean the essence of the proactive male and nurturing female in a unifying source.

CHAPTER 3

Consciousness

Consciousness and the Brain

As described in the previous chapter, scientists cannot explain how consciousness can occur in the brain. The reports of out of body experiences (OBE) indicate that consciousness does not appear to originate in the brain. Sometimes out of body experiences are called near death experiences (NDE). A great many reports have been made of continued consciousness and perceptual activity in persons who were considered technically dead or at least when their brains were not functioning. Individuals undergoing these experiences perceived events near or distant from their bodies. They viewed or reported such activities as: passing through a tunnel; overwhelming and profound love; a sense of purposefulness; being greeted by spiritual beings; and scenes of beauty. Some reported the presence of a guide. At such times, previously unknown relatives are also reported. In one remarkable instance, a totally blind person described the operating room and persons around her. Clinical reports are also available that describe individuals with large portions of their cortical lobes missing, but who continue to function normally in society. An interesting aspect of these reported experiences is that time seemed to acquire a spatial and timeless dimension.

Researchers have independently verified and reported a high degree of accuracy of the claims made. Reputable persons in all stations of life and education have reported such experiences. They also report being profoundly affected by their experiences in a spiritual manner.

A charming video report was made by a person who reported that as a result of his OBE experience, his "heart was on fire with love" (Ravi Rawat, BBC Video). He reports that he gave up his customary financial dealings and called his former associates to apologize for his activities in the past. He said that they answered his call with wariness, which turned into a stunned silence after his remarks. These reports strongly imply that the brain is a receiver of consciousness rather than its source. An extensive literature on this phenomenon can be found through Google search. An interesting and in depth review of OBE is also reported by Smed A. Jouni, Monroe Institute.

Out of body experiences are also reported to occur as a result of hypnotic trance and regression to earlier life times. Individuals have also experienced lucid dreams where they wake up inside their dream and experience an out of body experience. The propensity for the use of hallucinogens and drugs that induce hallucinations are also related to an escape from our everyday reality into another dimension of consciousness. Meditation, chants and other spiritually related activities may be related to inducing an altered state of consciousness. The premonitions that some people receive may be due to the external nature of our consciousness. It is also interesting to note, that although our body ages, our consciousness feels ageless. The nature and freshness of our consciousness never changes. It is why many people say, "I don't feel like the person that I see in the mirror". For the same reason some of our memories may remain vivid, because they are a part of the external source of our consciousness.

Although the body ages, our consciousness always feels young.

Consciousness the Source of Creation

It appears that the brain itself does not originate consciousness, but instead may be a receiver from God's greater consciousness. Indeed, how can consciousness be derived from flesh and blood? How could a piece of flesh create thought? How can our brain even possess love? It seems plausible to assume that our consciousness derives from and is part of God's greater consciousness and spirit that is within us. It is also a part of God's consciousness that sustains our bodies at every moment and propels our thoughts. We could not see, hear or think without his spirit and consciousness that emanates through our body. Our body and brain are only a vehicle for these functions and do not create them. Our consciousness is also the window of our spirit. As a result, consciousness is not a result, but the cause of life as we know it. Through God's consciousness, creativity continues as life manifests itself in us and his creations. It is for this reason, that consciousness is the basis of the world from which all living things are and were derived. This process continues today in our creation and re-creation at every moment.

> *God's consciousness is the basis of our creation.*

As God imagined the components of the world, he dispersed his consciousness and created them. He created a perfect world including the beauty of our flowers, trees and fauna. He also gave us the means with which to sustain our lives on earth. The food we eat, the lumber that we use to build your homes were imagined and created by him. As plants draw power from the sun, our body draws power from God's consciousness. His spirit is in every baby's smile, every person's tears and laughter. We are not flesh alone. Consciousness creates the elements of flesh, just as water is created from the oxygen and hydrogen in the air. As water becomes vapor, our consciousness continues after what we call death.

> *Consciousness is not the result of our brain; it is the cause of life as we know it.*

Our consciousness is here and now constrained to the physical being that is us. God's consciousness encompasses the past, present and future, and perhaps other dimensions that we are not aware of. That is why persons, who experience an out of body or near death experience, are freed from the dimension of time and see the past, as well as the future. As noted, love is also a part of God's consciousness that washes over people in a near death experience. Thus, we are also a part of God's love and consciousness and it may be argued that love is the only reality.

> *Your consciousness creates your body, propels your thoughts and sustains you in every instance.*

Halim Ozkaptan, Ph.D.

As God imagined us, he created us with his consciousness. He distributed sparks of himself, his consciousness, to us that empowers each human spirit. Each individual at their birth is essentially a rough sketch based upon the experiences of a previous lifetime. The specific personality, the "you" that you become, is developed through the creativity endowed in your consciousness. In a manner of speaking, you flesh and develop yourself through your own thoughts and beliefs. Like an artist, you add the color and details to the rough sketch that you are born with.[3] You develop yourself into the person that you are through the power of your consciousness and beliefs. Thus, you are a part of him and endowed by his creativity. We also continue his creations through our art, music and inventions.

Other Dimensions of Consciousness

Consciousness may also be a physical dimension or wave length not unlike the radio, TV, telephone and internet wave lengths. The latter require sources of generation and transmission through towers. God's consciousness, on the other hand, emanates from him and is the permeating and creative force of the universe and earth. It is everywhere at once without the temporal limitations of time. Moreover, any component of this wave length may affect other wave lengths in the future that it had interacted with before, independent of space, distance or time. Stewart Bell, a physicist, had introduced the concept of "entanglement" in quantum theory. It hypothesized that those tiny electron particles having once interacted would interact again, if one of the particles were activated regardless of the distance of their separation! Similarly, all of our spiritual natures may exist and interact simultaneously regardless of distance, if only we were sensitive and readily receptive to their existence.

We experience consciousness here and now in one dimension. Consciousness, however, may exist simultaneously in several dimensions, such as the past, present and future. This is not to say that there are other "wave lengths" of consciousness in another reality that may also exist, and perhaps, simultaneously with us that we do not

---

[3] Roberts, J. (1994). *The Nature of Personal Reality*. Novato, Calif: New World Library.

perceive. By virtue of our physical being, the body limits us to here and now and only the immediate moment. When we lose our physical body or die, we return to the full dimensions of our consciousness (past, present and future) without the constraint of the body. Hence, there is no death as we perceive it. Only the physical body dies. Our consciousness and spirit continue to exist. Without the body, the imposed restraints on consciousness are lost and we return to the unlimited full multi dimensions of God's consciousness. Plato had once said that we are prisoners of our body. The existence of an apparent greater consciousness implies that this is true. Schopenhauer had said that humans are paying the penalty of existence. Presumably, this may be due to our existence, or reincarnation, in body form.

The many out of body and near death experiences that have been reported, implies that mankind from the beginning of time had such experiences. The Tibetan Book of the Dead, as well as the Egyptian Book of the Dead, most likely had their genesis from such experiences, which led to their belief in a form of continued existence after physical death. Such experiences have resulted in a huge diversity of religious expression and cultural practices over the centuries. It has also led to countless cults, legitimate and otherwise, of 'seers", psychics, occultists and spiritualists. I was privileged to know a spiritualist by the name of Blanche Seder in the 1970's. She saw the past life times of some of my children and foresaw the untimely loss of one of them. In one instance, she knew I had taken a business trip by train to a certain city, when there was no possibility that she could have known this. There are spiritualists and "seers" with genuine gifts of clairvoyance of past life times and the future.

The implication that consciousness is imposed on the body indicates that consciousness similarly exists in all animals and creatures on earth and that they are equally a part of God's consciousness and plan. The theological and spiritual implications of this are profound, with issues of their spiritual nature, morality and in our treatment and responsibility for them.

CHAPTER 4

Your Spiritual Nature

Spiritual Source

Your spiritual nature derives from and is an intrinsic part of your consciousness and God's spirit. It is latent, however, until recognized and expressed by you. It is a reality, not hope or theory. It is a yearning and desire that waits to be awakened. Its development is your goal and ultimate fulfillment. It is the basis of your love, tears and laughter. It is the reason for your existence. Like your consciousness, your spirit is ever young and ageless. It has the power to lighten your heart and burdens and to give you relief from sickness and despair. Your spirit shares God's love and is that ever present feeling within you. When your sojourn on earth is completed, your spirit continues to reside in God's presence, spirit and love. Without your spirit and love, the world would be in chaos and could not exist. Without your spirit, you cannot know God or fulfill your potential. At birth, you are a creature of sweet innocence with a new and fresh challenge to develop your spiritual worth.

> *Your spiritual nature derives from and is part of your consciousness.*

If you believe that you are an accident of nature; that life is short, brutal and for the survival of the fittest; that old age is a time of decay; and that death is final so shall it be. You will live with a veil over your eyes and will view life darkly. Your happiness and prosperity will be limited and subject to random events in your life. You will be like a rudderless ship in the ocean subject to its waves. However, if you are aware of your living and eternal spirit, and seek its development, you will be sustained by its vitality and live a noble, vital and vigorous life. You will still be buffeted and challenged in life but will retain your control and achieve your goals and dreams.

> *Your life will flourish as you become aware of your living and eternal spirit.*

When your spirit is awakened, it will refresh your life, as cool water refreshes thirst. Your well-being will be accelerated and flourish. You will become sensitive to the spirits of the persons around you. You will be attracted to like-minded individuals without the trial and error of multiple interactions. Their character will be transparent to you during normal and casual meetings. You will not need to date and meet countless strangers to find the one that you will love. You will be repelled by cold and calculating individuals.

When your eyes are turned inward and veiled, you will be aware only of yourself and your own problems. With awareness of your spiritual nature, your eyes are turned outward, your life is put in perspective, and you become sensitive and attuned to others. Your spirit is an untapped source of love waiting to be released. Through your awareness of it, your development is accelerated. It is the least understood part of human nature. It is the source of your goodwill, initiative and willingness to strive and engage in life. It is the basis of your faith. Your spiritual nature is the core and essence of your life.

> *Your spirit refreshes your life, as cool water refreshes your thirst.*

Spiritual Challenge

We were not given a portion of God's spirit without being held responsible for it. We are accountable for this gift. The world was not created to be rendered asunder by your avarice and pride. Guilt and remorse are reflections of its abuse. Flesh has no feeling. It is our living spirit that suffers. Because of this gift, our responsibility is enormous. Life is a challenge to test your worthiness for the gift of life that you have received. Your purpose on earth is to grow in spiritual value and become worthy of God's love.

We are accountable for the spirit that we have received.

We are here to learn how to live without the temptations of greed, jealousy, lust and other vices. Do you give fair measure in your business and daily transactions? Do you honor your responsibilities to your family, colleagues and subordinates? Do you honor and value your spouse and treat him or her with respect, love and devotion? Do you greet and treat your fellow man with goodwill? Do you endeavor and persevere, despite obstacles, to realize and develop your potential? The development of your moral worth is the reason and purpose of your life. Your ultimate goal is to develop your spiritual nature and become worthy of God's love.

Your life on earth is a morality play where all of your actions will be evaluated and judged by your creator. Your spiritual challenge is to grow in value and moral worth. The key challenge in this morality play is to never injure another individual through word, deed or action. Every deed and thought of your life will impact upon your spiritual and moral worth. Every aspect of your life is "influenced" by your moral worth. Your experiences and reactions are a test of your moral worth. You have been given a unique challenge. It is your responsibility to grow, develop spiritually, and become worthy of the spirit with which you have been endowed.

Life is a morality play.

Your spirit will be challenged and developed over many of your lifetimes. You will be challenged to live in harmony and love with your fellow man and to live without the temptations of greed, jealousy, lust and other vices. You will have many failures and temptations. Events will happen in your life for a reason. You are not a random victim. Those with a good heart will remain unharmed or "protected" during their life time. They need not fear the future. Every negative act you do will return to you until you learn empathy and gain love. It is not an easy process and may take many lifetimes. People who do not live in harmony and love with others will face two consequences. The first is that every negative or positive thing that they do to another, they are also doing to themselves. The second is that it will shape their character and the future events that will befall them.

Halim Ozkaptan, Ph.D.

What you do to others you are doing to yourself.

Through belief in yourself and your spiritual nature, you must endeavor to burn out, control and remove the dross and impurities in your life. It is like burning out the imperfections of gold to bring out its purity. The process is not easy. Do not lose that sweet spirit through sinful acts. Do not let it slip away and become a hard and cynical person. You are here to work out any imperfections and not add to them. Every action in your life influences your spiritual development and moral worth. Your moral worth is the sum of your behavior and actions based on love, thoughtfulness and consideration of others. As you recognize and develop your spirit, your life flourishes. As you ignore it, the fullness of your life diminishes. Your personal development, your interactions with others and your loved ones are reflections of and the result of your spiritual behavior.

Your spiritual journey on earth will not be easy. Nor is it intended to be easy. You will be challenged in all aspects of your life. Your actions, or lack of actions, will be a measure of your moral worth. Your life will entail many failures and pain. There will be a constant struggle between your best and worst selves. Your happiness and contentment on earth will depend upon your success in this struggle. Unless you persevere in your spiritual challenge, your well-being and happiness will remain elusive. Each of us has been given a unique challenge. People and events will come in and out of your life for support, or as a challenge, to help you grow and become worthy of returning to God's presence. Unless you recognize and persevere in your spiritual challenge, your well-being and happiness will remain elusive.

Your spiritual journey on earth will not be easy.

Do not regret your past failures and actions. You are a different and better person today than you were before. Your spirit has grown as a result of your trials and responses to them. Look forward to new trials, opportunities and certain joys to come. You will be a better person in the future as your spiritual journey continues. Your past lives have contributed to your development. Your experiences in this life continue to do so. Do not look back, except to change the thoughts and conditions in the past that may have contributed to your failures and illnesses. You will recycle on this earth until you learn to live with grace, love and goodwill.

Spiritual Relationships

Our spirits, with those of others, are interconnected and influence each other in subtle ways. There is an invisible hand ever present in our lives that is expressed through the knowing and unknowing conscious and subconscious mediation of others. From across the world or across the street, your spirits can sense each other. How many times have you thought of a friend when the phone rings? How often do you have the same thoughts as your spouse, or friend, before they are expressed? You can also sense the presence of your departed ones. Leave your hearts and minds open to this. Lack of belief and faith prevents such communication. If you are open to and accept your spirituality, you can sense each other's thoughts, as well as sense the presence of your departed loved ones. In effect, it is as if all the spirits are near you, regardless of the degree of your physical separation. Ultimately, everyone is spiritually interconnected.

Your spirits can sense each other despite any degree of separation.

The spiritual bond between parents and their children is one of the strongest bonds. It is a function of like souls attracting each other through the centuries. Even when a parent dies, children continue to feel a sense of personal loss and abandonment. Adopted children, despite their love for their adoptive parents, also long to know and have an affinity for their birth parents.

Events will also happen in your life for reasons unknown to you. They may be for your benefit or loss. The statement that there are no coincidences is not an idle one. Due to preordained spiritual goals, interventions beyond your understanding can occur. Those with goodwill are aided in their deepest desires, such as when they pursue an education or buy a house. Interventions will also occur to save the worthy from the worst consequences of their own actions or from potential accidents. Those who abuse their spirit are frustrated from success in achieving their own desires and plans.

There are no coincidences.

Listen also to your intuition. It draws from your eternal spirit and the associated spirits who surround you. It represents the accumulated knowledge of your spirit and former experiences. It will try to break through during your times of need, and indeed will alert you in time of danger. Your perception, intuitions and premonitions are a function of your spiritual nature.

Listen to your intuitions.

The Soul

Our spiritual nature is part of God's spirit waiting to be awakened. It is developed as part of our actions due to our free will. Our soul represents the flowering of our spirit. As our spiritual and moral worth grows, our soul matures and blossoms. The maturing of our soul represents the flowering of God's love. As a rose bud is to a rose, our spirit is to our soul. Our developed soul is the ultimate fulfillment of God's love.

Without good works and moral worth, your spirit is dormant. As a result, the development of your soul lays fallow without its fulfillment in love. As you control your negative behavior and grow in spiritual worth, you add to the development of your soul. Your soul is the burning and growing edge of your spirit. It is the heart, and essence of your living and eternal spirit. You can sense your soul in quiet times of contemplation when you are with your loved ones, or surrounded by the beauty of nature. Your soul is not rational. It is pure love and goodwill.

Your soul is the embodiment of love.

At birth your soul has a certain value and level of development. Relative to this value, your life on earth will be circumscribed between certain boundaries and events. These boundaries and events are intended to guide and influence the development of your soul. As described in a later Chapter, these events will be both positive and negative. Good and bad things will happen to influence the development of your soul. As you learn to control your passions and actions, your soul continues its development. As your spiritual self grows in value, you will draw closer to God's spirit and love in your soul. A person with an advanced soul shines and emanates love and goodwill. It is reflected in their eyes and smile. Love flourishes in them as a result of their maturing soul. They radiate in the presence of others. Your developed soul is the ultimate result and goal of your journeys on earth. It is that perfect place in you that our creator waits, for so that it can eventually join with him in love.

Your consciousness and spiritual nature are passing and transient events that are intended for the development of your soul. Your soul is permanent and exists forever as you transition between life times. Ultimately, when the development of your soul is complete, you will return permanently to his essence and being. At that time, you will be in a total state of bliss and grace. Your soul will exist through eternity in his presence. Your sojourns on earth will have ended and you will no longer need to return to a physical body. At that time, you will be one of God's angels and surrogates.

Your soul is permanent and exists for ever.

Evil

You may ask, if we are part of God's spirit why are many people cruel, selfish and evil? How could it be? It is because with a portion of God's spirit, we also have free will. We can make our own good and bad decisions! It is a paradox. If we have a portion of God's spirit and consciousness, then we have the power of creativity and freedom of choice. As a result, a lot of mischief and cruelty is possible. But this does not mean that man is evil and that he is born with sin. No, it only means that man can make spiritually bad decisions. Their accomplishments, however, will be built on quicksand. Their spirits will exist in a state of turmoil and doubt. It is our responsibility to use our free will for love and good works, so that we can be worthy of God's love and grace. This is the central message of all religions. As love is the only reality, evil is the absence of love.

Cruelty is the result of free will to choose one's actions.

CHAPTER 5

Manifestations of Your Spiritual Nature and Consciousness

Many of our thoughts, feelings, love and events in our life are manifestations of our spiritual nature. Be alert to these feelings and emotions as expressions of your spiritual nature. Become tuned to the reality of your spiritual nature.

Love

Love is the ultimate manifestation of God's reality and your spiritual nature. It is the essence of your soul and God's presence. It is that indescribable feeling of love between parents and their children and between lovers. It is the ultimate goal you strive for in your spiritual development and journey to become one with God. The discussion of love is expanded upon in Chapter 7.

Love is the only reality.

Faith

Faith is central to your spiritual nature. It is a belief in God and that you are not an accident of nature and subject to capricious forces until a meaningless death. You are not an accident of fate, but a creation of your creator and his greater plan. Have faith that you are endowed with God's consciousness and spirit, and that you are here to test and demonstrate your moral worth. Have faith that you are not a random creation, but a part of God's plan with the responsibility to grow, prosper and to develop your natural and endowed skills. Have faith that you are here for a purpose, and that you will be challenged to use your skills and talents. You are also part of a larger plan to create and support your family and to advance society.

Faith is also an impetus to persevere and to fulfill your responsibilities. It cannot be vicarious or passive. Faith helps a person to attenuate anxiety and fear through the belief that they are not subject to capricious external forces. It also offers the consolation of an eternal life in the hereafter. Similarly, if God is viewed as a metaphor of spiritual potential in the human heart, a spirit living a human life, the fear of death is reduced. Through these and similar mechanisms, faith reduces the effects of fear and contributes to a person's perseverance. Faith in your spiritual nature, in yourself, unencumbered by negative thoughts and actions, supports your resolve and your efforts to attain your goals and maintain your spiritual worth.

Faith without practice is empty and without redemption.

Goodwill

Goodwill is the expression of love and is the ability to deal with people with an open and accepting heart. It is to be concerned for the welfare of others and their well-being. Your expression of goodwill to others is one of the most powerful indications of your moral and spiritual worth. It is the hallmark of a "good person". It is also one of the important contributors to your personal success, as it attracts others who sense it, and reciprocate with concern for your well-being and success. Your goodwill reflects your spiritual nature and God's love which creates it. If you are suspicious of others, uncharitable, cold and indifferent, people will sense it and not voluntarily support you. Your goodwill supports and nourishes your spiritual nature, conscious thoughts, faith, and beliefs. Be courteous, pleasant and cheerful when dealing with others. Your warmth will attract people to you. Your goals are more likely to be supported. When you are under stress or difficulty, people are more likely to come to your aid. With lack of goodwill and courtesy, people will not support you.

Desire

Unless you set desires or goals for yourself, they cannot materialize. Faith and goodwill play an important role in the realization of your desires. Faith releases the power of your spirit. Without faith, your desires cannot materialize from thought to reality. It transforms the desire into a reality similar to a film negative that creates a positive picture. This process, however, depends upon your goodwill and good heart. Lack of goodwill can block or short-circuit the power of your spirit. Without goodwill, neither desire nor faith can function (Roberts, 1994). Thus, desire, faith and goodwill together are the "magical" qualities that focus and accelerate the realization of your deepest desires and goals.

> *Faith and goodwill are the magical qualities that focus and accelerate the achievement of your goals.*

Dreams

The fact that our consciousness is imposed by God opens a wide door to speculation about the nature of dreams. As you work out your spiritual life during the day, you continue to resolve issues in your dreams and subconscious. Falling asleep is similar to being on the other side when your consciousness is freed from your body, as in death. Time is a frame work for our growth on earth. In dreams, we dip into our greater consciousness, spiritual nature and distant past to resolve daily and past issues. Dreams are quickly forgotten, as they are not a part of your normal consciousness. Your dreams think that your waking self is a dream. There is more to the mystery of life than can be revealed by this book alone.

Hope

Hope draws from the spirit. Hope represents your desire to grow, achieve your goals and to succeed. It seeks redemption from your mistakes and failures and the desire to improve. It is the desire for better things to come. During difficult times, never give up hope for better days. Do not live with regrets for past occurrences. You are no longer the same person. New opportunities and joys wait for you. To say "I can't" in the face of new opportunities is a denial of yourself and your eternal spirit.

Never lose hope for a loved one, due to their failures or shortcomings. It dishonors them by not giving them credit for having the ability to change. Hope is a form of charity that overlooks their faults and weaknesses. As they face their problems and grow in spiritual value, they become a different person. Give them credit for that and accept it in yourself. Hope is like faith. It releases the power of your spirit. If you are sick, hope and belief in your recovery will help to assure it. Despair will only help to promote your illness.

Prayer

Through your prayers, you release the power of your living and eternal spirit that resides in you. The effectiveness of your prayers depends upon a good heart and your good deeds. They are thwarted by a self-serving and malicious heart. When you are moved by or need his spirit, pray to God from wherever you may be. Before there were formal religions, people still prayed to God in their quiet moments. When a person prays, the contemplation and focusing of consciousness, and the power of suggestion, helps the prayer to become its own answer.

> *Prayer is its own answer.*

In addition to the great cathedrals and places of worship, let the beauty of the world around you, such as the forest, the meadow and the seaside, serve as your cathedral. Prayer also puts you in contact with the larger spiritual world of your loved ones and those who have passed on. When you think of them you draw them near to you and gain their strength and support. When in a stressful situation, in addition to prayer, bring your loved ones and those departed to mind. They will support you spiritually and emotionally. You will gain strength and as a minimum, your self-confidence will be lifted.

> *"God willing" is not an empty phrase.*

Thoughts

As our thoughts are the result of our consciousness, they have the power of our consciousness to create our reality. In a very real sense, thoughts are "things" and part of our reality. They are the guiding edge of our consciousness. Our living and eternal spirit responds to our thoughts to create our reality. For this reason, you must dare to dream. It will guide your reality. Your dreams and desires will ultimately materialize. You also create many of your own illnesses through your negative thoughts. Often your imagination is fed by the many medical advertisements that you are exposed to in the media. They help to create your symptoms. The power of most medicines is your belief in them. Believe instead in your own health and well-being. Maintain a positive attitude toward yourself, your goals, health and capabilities. Watch your thoughts. If you think that you are sickly, or unworthy of success, you will create that reality. Do not identify with anything that you do not wish to become, such as very aged and sickly people. To do so, will draw you to that reality.

You are free from harm except for your negative thoughts.

Do not live with fear or anxiety. It will limit your opportunities. You are basically free from harm, except for your negative thoughts and own behavior. When you are fearful and afraid of danger, you will attract it to you. Lesser persons with evil intent will sense your fears, and will be drawn to you to oblige your fears. Your self-confidence will help to repel danger and harm. You are not a victim. Fear only the consequences of your own thoughts or negative behaviors.

Thoughts are "things" and create your reality.

Beliefs

Your beliefs influence your thoughts. Your beliefs about yourself, other people, religion and politics define you. Your beliefs about yourself, affects your feelings of self-worth and self-confidence. Your beliefs about others, determine your interactions, prejudices and ability to effectively deal with them. Parental attitudes can affect your beliefs about yourself. Their encouragement and confidence in you can have profound effects. Think about the unconscious negative beliefs that you may hold about yourself. Root them out. They can unconsciously hold you back. Your beliefs guide your thoughts, or act in concert with them to create your perceptions. If you believe that you are sick or unworthy, so shall you be. Your beliefs about others, will also affect your dealings with them. If you are trusting, this will facilitate your interactions with others. Suspicion on your part, however, will limit openness and goodwill, and can also affect how others perceive and accept you.

Your beliefs guide your thoughts.

Self-Suggestion

Your daily thoughts and self-suggestions also carry the creativity of your consciousness and influence your reality. The power of your consciousness and spiritual nature respond to and "materialize" the suggestion. The power of suggestion is demonstrated by hypnosis. The hypnotist hypnotizes you quickly by focusing your attention on the suggestions that he gives you. By the same means, you hypnotize yourself slowly and gradually each day with your own thoughts. The power of hypnosis, voodoo, acupuncture and many traditional medicines lie in the power of suggestion.

You hypnotize yourself with your daily thoughts.

CHAPTER 6

Life's Purpose

Spiritual Development

Life is a test of your moral worth. You are challenged to contribute to your moral development and atone for deeds in your present or former life. Life is also a gift. It is not intended, however, to be a bed of roses but one of challenge and growth. Life is full of pitfalls and betrayals. Accidents can happen, bad luck occurs, compounded by mistakes and poor judgment. Whether born rich or poor, life will come at you as in a storm. It will assault and challenge you with loss and despair. There will be a series of challenges to overcome; whether it is sickness, loss of a job, marital and financial problems, crime, fraud or the demands of the job or school. There will be failures, including school dropouts and divorce. Poor personal habits will affect your personal health such as lack of exercise, poor diet, obesity, smoking and drugs.

Sin and crime may occur due to the lack of will to adhere to your better instincts and impulses. As a result, the realization of your potential, opportunity and investments will fail or be lost. How will you react? Will you give up? Self-pity, drugs and alcohol are the easy way out. Or will you lick and bind your wounds and persevere? A person either perseveres to overcome their challenges, or takes the easy way out. By persevering, whether successful or not, they develop their character and demonstrate their moral worth.

Life will come at you as in a storm.

A person is a failure only when they do not defy and attempt to overcome the events that befall them. To persevere and lose is far better than succumbing to or accepting the adverse events in your life. Only then, win or lose, has a person demonstrated their heroic nature. It is how you face and deal with life's challenges that determine your character and your ultimate success in life. Will you persevere in difficulty? Will you be patient in adversity and be modest in success? Or will you take the easy way out at your own expense and negatively impact your character? It will determine the outcome and the nature of your character and self-worth. Your spiritual development, in part, depends upon how you handle life's inevitable setbacks.

Your character is your destiny.

Some individuals who suffer severe setbacks in their goals can be traumatized and give up. Rather than dwell on their loss, many overcome it and continue with their lives. Many persons have handicaps such as blindness or physical deformities that are cruel to see or contemplate. Jeff Bauman, a marathon runner, who lost both his legs in the Boston terrorist attack of April 2013, wrote a book about his experience. He said, "I saw the bomber. He took my legs, but he didn't break me. It only made me stronger". He became stronger because of his misfortune. This is a good example of perseverance and inner strength to overcome adversity and hardship without complaint. Such people are not defined by their limitations, nor do they become "professional victims", relying on the sympathy and support of others. They celebrate their spirit through perseverance and adjustment. They become stronger. They find more contentment in life than those who give up, or those who may have gained success without the benefit of their own efforts, or on the backs of others.

To succumb to stress, doubt and outside pressure has serious personal consequences. Such individuals become pitiful, self-indulgent, and give up. It is better to try and fail, as it still develops one's fortitude and perseverance. Those who continue to strive, despite obstacles, are tempered, unbowed and honor themselves by their effort. They become less fearful of known and unknown events in their life. They achieve a new understanding of themselves. They have tested and demonstrated their potential and personal fortitude. They fulfill their destiny.

After every difficulty there is relief.

Self-Realization

You are also endowed by your creator with capabilities to be developed and fulfilled. Self-realization is viewed by Jung (1964) as man's highest goal: "... the full realization of the potential of his individual self". Through self-realization, the individual discovers and develops his own capabilities. In early history, war between two individuals was seen as a way to develop courage and resourcefulness and to accentuate their egos through self-realization. An extreme view of this principle is reflected in Mayan behavior (600-800 A.D.). They would sacrifice the wining captain of a football game. He was deemed worthy of sacrifice, at the winning stroke of his life (Campbell (1987). Campbell states that the basic motif of the universal hero's challenge is to evolve from the state of psychological immaturity to the courage of self-responsibility, assurance and ultimately, the adventure of being alive. He describes a long journey to be taken with many trials. Can you overcome the dangers? Do you have the courage, the knowledge, the capacity to enable you to succeed? Through self-realization, the individual discovers his own capabilities.

In their quest for self-realization, an individual aspires to grow, develop and fulfill their potential. When they add value to themselves through personal development, it contributes to their self-realization. When their accomplishments are recognized by others, it supports their self-esteem. As their perceived value increases, they have more incentive to "persevere as a person" and to sustain their image. This leads to increase their self-worth which underlies self-esteem. These qualities help an individual to resist adversity. It is reflected in the tenacious will of some individuals who survive, despite the worst of circumstances. Their pride helps to resist events which would otherwise take it away. This is reflected in what the philosopher Spinoza referred to as "...striving to persevere in our own being". In summary, a person's self-realization reduces to a moral and volitional issue. A person perseveres as a matter of conscience, in order not to tarnish what is important to their own being as a person and their relationship with others.

> *Through self-realization an individual aspires to grow and realize their potential.*

Goethe had said that the godhead, or striving toward the divine, is effective in the becoming and the changing, not in what already has become and set fast. This point is developed further by Campbell (1987) who states: "But the goal of your quest for knowledge of yourself is to be found at that burning point in yourself, that becoming thing in yourself, which is innocent of the goods and evils of the world as already become, and therefore desire less and fearless. That is the condition of the warrior going into battle with perfect courage. That is life in movement. That is the essence on the mysticism of war". He further states that: "The conquest of fear yields the courage of life. That is the cardinal initiation of every heroic adventure –fearlessness and achievement".

> *The conquest of fear yields the courage of life.*

Campbell further notes that the adventure of life implies danger, like the edge of a razor, where control of emotion and enthusiasm is necessary to avoid disaster. A person who does his duty is stronger because of it. He has been tested, and found not wanting in his own heart which helps to bring out his heroic qualities. Ultimately, the achievement of heroic deeds leads to a transformation in the individual, with benefits to others by the example set. The hero's quest evokes character, as he learns about himself. Each of the great religions teaches that the trials of the hero's journey are a significant part of life; that there is no reward without sacrifice. The ultimate trial is when we no longer think of ourselves and self-preservation, but give or sacrifice for others. Heroism, like courage, is a result of both self-realization and sacrifice for others. Through self-realization the hero discovers his own capabilities. That is the cardinal initiation of every heroic adventure –fearlessness and achievement.

> *The ultimate trial is when we no longer think of ourselves and sacrifice for others.*

Loss of Hope and Suicide

Suicide results from the failure to persevere in the face of challenges and the loss of hope. While not a sin, it is a lack of faith that events will not change to a person's advantage. Suicide interrupts their spiritual development. They falsely pre-judge the future and miss unknown joys and opportunities. Self-pity, punishment of another, sacrifice for loved ones are not an excuse to end one's life. Many other people would trade their problems for the problems that are being escaped through suicide.

Those who put conditions on life, that are not met, are prone to suicide. They must realize that their goals will not be met on their schedule or time table. Their desires will work out in due time, on a schedule unknown to them. Despite their desires and hopes, only God will determine when they will be achieved. Those who take their own lives will dwell in the regret of their decision until they return to earth to make amends to those they have affected. They may face new and harder challenges to compensate and atone for their former action. They may lose their life unwillingly at an early age, to understand the value of the gift they had formerly and willingly forfeited.

Do not put conditions on life.

To those who are contemplating suicide, do not deceive yourself by temporary and passing problems. It is a selfish act to those you will leave behind. It will deprive them of your love and support. It accomplishes nothing and punishes your loved ones. Do not voluntarily end your life. You will learn to regret it as you understand the import of your action on others and atone for it in the hereafter and during other lifetimes. After every difficult there is relief.

CHAPTER 7

Love and Relationships

Love

The essence of God is love. The only reality is love. All other aspects of the world are temporal. Love dwells in our spirit and is a part of God's love and reality. When someone is attracted to you, they are attracted to the elegant and graceful characteristics of your personality and indeed the warmth of your spirit. This recognition touches your desire to be recognized and appreciated. It is the recognition of your value. You react by being attracted to and loving that person for seeing the value in you! In turn, your loving reaction to them endorses and recognizes their value. This is the awakening of love, the mutual recognition and enhancement of each other's value. That value is the love and goodwill in each other's spiritual nature.

Adding value to a person is the basis of love.

Your love is sustained by the admiration of your lover. Their love is sustained by your admiration of him or her. Your being loved adds to your self-realization. Your spirituality blossoms by being in love. Your mutual admiration contributes to each other's self-realization and value. It thrives when this admiration is mutually sustained by word and deed. Benefits flow to each of you as a result of your love for each other.

Your spirit blossoms when in love.

Love has several stages of increasing development and depth. The first occurs in youth, when a young boy or girl becomes excited for being noticed. It is their first recognition of 'self" from a source outside of themselves. There is excitement and anticipation of events to come. It is free of a sexual component although it may be explored. The second stage is a strong attraction between young men and women. It includes a desire to share experiences, with sex as a byproduct. This does not include the lust that may motivate some individuals for no more than a single night. The third is a deepening need to share experiences together, and to be recognized as a couple. It may lead to becoming engaged to get married. The fourth stage is a bonding of spirits where desires and goals become one with unity of purpose. It leads to marriage with shared values and goals and to having children. In the early stages, love starts with words. It is the necessary vehicle to learn about each other. Ultimately, true love is expressed without words and by simple glances and gestures. It includes holding each other close, caressing each other, and letting your emotions and feelings flow between you. These moments come closest to feeling the spiritual aspect of love.

True love is expressed and felt without words.

The final stage occurs when you live for and sacrifice for your loved one. The welfare of your loved one is more important than your own welfare and happiness. At this stage, you anticipate each other's thoughts. There is a blending of your feelings and consciousness. You are "beyond love". It is the stage when sacrifice for each other is more important than your own needs or safety. It is a selfless love that awakens your better self. You become more than yourself. Your loved one is your passion and fulfillment. Their happiness is your happiness. He, or she, is a reflection of God's love and grace in your life. At this stage, you have found the spiritual face of God and his love.

You are beyond love, when you live for and sacrifice for your loved one.

Marriage

To marry for any reason less than love is a mistake, if not a sin. Your choice of a partner should be compelling. Do not marry in haste. Do not settle or rationalize your choice. If you have to think, or rationalize your choice, do not do it. If you are being pressured into marriage, do not do it. Any reason less than love will end in failure. Your doubts and motives must become clear in your mind. Unless you marry for love and devotion and for the care and well-being of your loved one, you are committing a mistake. If you marry for sex, you will eventually experience disgust and contempt. If you marry for money, you will work for it and earn it as if you were engaged in an odious job. You will also lose self-respect, dignity and eventually will be humiliated by your partner. If you marry for power or position, you will find emptiness and self-contempt. You will become vainglorious and without respect for your partner. Your life will become an empty shell.

Your choice of a mate should be compelling.

While love exists between lovers, friends and families, its home is in marriage. Marriage is the most complex and rewarding form of human relationships. It is your foremost spiritual challenge and test, and a test of your moral fiber and value as a person. Can you indeed "cherish, honor and obey"? Those who marry advance their spiritual development and come closer to God's spirit of love, through personal responsibility for each other.

Marriage is the home of love.

Marriage is the center, heart and crucible of your life's spiritual interactions. You will have embarked on a spiritual journey. It is a journey based on hope and a promise. It is the hope of an enduring love and the promise of lasting devotion to each other. It is the crucible for every good and bad deed between two people. Your spouse is your spiritual partner. It is a critical test of your spiritual worth. Honor and value your spouse and treat each other with respect, love and devotion. To have a true and enduring love and marriage in your life is one of life's greatest blessings.

Marriage is a hope and a promise.

Marry well. You pick up each other's personalities and spirit which become a part of you and strengthen you. You accelerate each other's spiritual growth and grow closer together. Through marriage alone, you complete at least one half of your spiritual goals and development. To some degree, you meld your spirits.

Marriage is a spiritual journey.

One of life's primary goals is spiritual awakening, value and development. It is achieved and sustained through love and marriage. As a result, it is important to find someone at your level of moral and spiritual development. Do not be so blinded by love that you lose sight of your lover's character. You will attribute and project many noble qualities and characteristics to your lover that may not exist. He or she is the realization of your dreams and will benefit automatically from your desires and wishful perceptions. Listen to the advice and perceptions of others who may not be so blinded.

Be alert and sensitive to your potential partner's character. Love predisposes good character, or at least equivalent character and behavior, in your partner. Stealing, betrayal and deception, for example, are inconsistent with fidelity and devotion. Loss of respect can quickly develop between persons of different character and value systems. Make no mistake, would you respect someone with a value system that is less than your own or in conflict with yours? In the greater scheme of things, the good are intended for the good. Differences in education or socioeconomic status are much less important than similarity in moral background.

Seek moral equivalency in your partner.

Sex

Sexual desire is the only part of your life where you do not have free will. It is not a choice but an irresistible urge for physical release in order to assure the propagation of mankind. Our motivation for procreation is necessary to assure the continuity, purpose of life and our re-occurrence on earth. Sex emanates from the body. Love from the spirit. Sex finds its ultimate expression in love. Aside from the differences in sexual organs, men and women are the same, with the same spiritual challenges, emotions and capabilities. However, men and women are irresistible to each other. Many stray from the bonds of a relationship or marriage. Sexual activity with anyone other than the one you love and have married can damage your relationship through guilt and loss of trust. While it can affect your relationship, do not let it destroy it. Avoid promiscuity. Protect your reputation and your health from disease. Do not sell it for a "cheap coin." Your self-control, discrimination and moderation are part of your spiritual challenge.

Sex finds its ultimate expression in love.

Homosexuality

Our spiritual nature and soul have no gender. It is neither male nor female. At birth our bodies become either male or female, to enable human propagation. As a male, we typically take on an assertive nature. As a female, our nurturing side blossoms. The differences in our sexual characteristics attract us to each other. It is love that leads to the desire for marriage as well as the growth of our spiritual nature.

Spiritual attraction and love, however, are not limited to differences in our sexual organs. Some individuals are attracted to the same sex. A same sex relationship is another avenue for spiritual attraction, love and growth. Although it appears unnatural, it is not a choice, but is predetermined by ones spiritual orientation to the same sex. It is a spiritual attraction and it is not a sin. It is one of the many permutations of our spiritual nature. Love also follows in this situation for the same reasons as conventional heterosexual love.

Homosexuality is a spiritual attraction to the same sex.

Same sex couples are also seeking love and self-realization. They are partners in life in the truest sense. Their motivation in marriage is love and companionship similar to heterosexual couples, not sex alone. Those who oppose same sex marriage are missing the point. They dwell on the sexual component rather than the love between two people. The dynamics involved are no more or less than the conventional attraction between persons of the opposite sex. The homosexual person is also a member of the human family. They too are on a voyage of self-discovery, challenge, personal and spiritual growth. They should have the same right to the safe guards and privileges of marriage. Love them as you would love anyone else.

Same sex couples are also seeking love and self-realization.

Do not scorn the homosexual person. It only reveals the doubt about your own sexuality and inclination. You may be condemning what you fear in yourself. The homosexual person tempers the extreme characteristics of the heterosexual person. Some adopt homosexual stereotypes as they struggle with their conflicting identity. Unfortunately, some parents may have difficulty accepting the sexual orientation of their child. They cannot change it. They should simply be happy, if they have a good child.

CHAPTER 8

Why Bad Things Happen

As described in Chapter 6, you will face many challenges. Although a paradox, bad things will also happen for good reasons. Good things will happen to test your reaction to them. Life's experiences, as a result, will ultimately be a balance between gain and loss to develop your moral worth. Such events will occur periodically throughout your life. If all the bad things in life happened at the same time, you would be overwhelmed by despair. If all the good things were to happen at the same time, you would be overwhelmed by ecstasy.

On many occasions, you will be challenged by adverse situations. You reputation will be demeaned. You will lose loved ones. Opportunities will be lost. Your health may fail. No one is immune. It is not a result of bad or good luck. Despite your resolve and best efforts, it is a part of life and the challenges you are destined to face.

You will be tested by life's challenges.

As described below, hardship will occur to test you and to accelerate your growth and spiritual development. It will occur when you are being used as a deterrent to thwart lesser men in their sinful and evil acts. It will occur when you are an innocent victim of someone's malfeasance, or for your own atonement. You will never understand the reasons for many of these events. However, you will receive no adversity greater than you can bear. Persevere, in such times, there are immediate and long range reasons for every hardship. Through hardship, and your perseverance, you are being transformed into a better and stronger person.

You will have no adversity greater than you can bear.

Hardship as a Challenge

You will be tested by hardship to challenge your resolve and character and to bring out your latent capabilities. It is the better person who is so tested and strengthened for future challenges. It is a part of your spiritual development and a test of your reported "mettle". Did you fail on an important test or task? Did someone falsely accuse you about some negative event? Did you lose a business opportunity? By such adversities, your character is tempered and hardened and prepared for other challenges that may come your way.

Through hardship you are challenged to become a stronger person.

Defeat and loss will temper your pride and any vainglorious attitudes that you may harbor. While you will regret your loss, you will have other compensating successes. Misfortune will strengthen your compassion for others. Some seriously disabled individuals overcome crippling limitations. They celebrate their spirit and serve as an inspiration for others. There is often good in what you otherwise would see as failure or loss. Have faith. There are reasons for the events in your life that you may eventually understand in the larger scheme of your life. Honored is the person who accepts their loss or defeat gracefully.

After every difficulty there is relief.

Hardship as a Deterrent

Unfortunately, human interactions involve the worst and the best characteristics of people. Some of you, however, when unfairly demeaned or "assaulted" may be playing a role in a larger spiritual plan. You may be serving as a deterrent to block the adverse actions of persons of lesser character. A person with character reflects the lesser person's imperfections and enhances their insecurity, jealousy and self-doubt. The lesser person will gratuitously try to injure such a person through lies about their character, or by other means. The offended person through their responses, and perhaps the support of others, may be serving as a foil upon which the offending person will be blocked or thwarted. As a nation must defend itself to stop, or change the behavior of aggressors, so do some people knowingly or unknowingly serve as a deterrent to block malicious people.

> *Some of you will serve as foils to deter the transgressions of others.*

Yes, good people will suffer loss and hurt, but they will eventually realize that they are free of harm in the larger picture. They will begin to wonder what fate or loss their offenders may have brought upon themselves. They may eventually witness the retribution that their attackers receive. Hold no animosity. The hatred of others will bounce off you and affect only them. It takes two hands to clap, and two people to sustain hatred. Despite the difficulties you may face, there are kindred spirits who watch over you. In times of need, they will materialize to aid you. It will include many people that you barely know. They will intervene and come into your life at critical moments throughout your life to help you.

> *When in need, support will come from unexpected places.*

Hardship to Prevent a Greater Loss

Hardship may occur to prevent a greater unknown future loss, or tragedy, that would otherwise befall you. You may have a minor accident in order to avoid a larger tragedy such as a plane crash. The loss of a desired financial transaction could be to prevent an unforeseen bankruptcy in the future. However unforeseen and tragic an event may be, it may not be an entirely random occurrence. There are mysterious and unfathomable forces at work to protect you. What sometimes could be viewed as bad luck, such as having been caught in an earthquake or flood, may also be attributable to your spiritual attraction to the challenges of that particular area or situation.

Halim Ozkaptan, Ph.D.

Hardship as Atonement

Some of the misfortune that you experience in life could also be a form of atonement for your actions in your present or former life. A present physical deformity could be due to an injury that you caused to another in a former life. Poverty could result due to your impoverishment of others. Sooner or later, you will atone for your negative and adverse actions, now or in a future life. If a man blinds a person in this life, he is destined to be blind in this or the next life. Atonement is not for punishment, retribution or revenge, but to help that person understand and feel the consequences of his or her former deed. It will be a means to teach empathy and how it feels to be treated, hurt or cheated in the same way.

> *Atonement is intended to each empathy for one's former negative actions.*

Our spiritual development includes atonement for negative and sinful actions in our present and past lives. As part of our atonement, we live our lives between predetermined boundaries of success and failure, gain and loss. The implication is that regardless of how hard we try, our lives to some extent are predetermined due to past actions. We are coping with our limitations, faults, adversaries and atonement for past sins. It is part of our spiritual journey to achieve spiritual perfection, love and eternal life. The significant events in our life may not be random occurrences.

> *Our gains and losses are kept within spiritually predetermined boundaries.*

Tragedies will also happen to good people. How does one explain the mass suffering of innocents in the world such as 40,000 young men being killed in one day at the battle of Somme during WW I, the extermination camps during WWII, and the mass loss of life in Hiroshima and Nagasaki in Japan when an atomic bomb was released? Their real and apparent suffering, however, is instantly relieved by passing into the ultimate reality of God's presence where they immediately find love and acceptance. The brutality of life can only be explained by their redemption in love in God's presence. It is those who are responsible for their suffering and death that have injured their souls and who will repent. Their atonement waits for them in this world and the next. It is the victims that find peace and love, not the perpetrators whose trials have only just begun. God's books and ledgers are eventually balanced slowly and finely in the morality play of life.

God grinds slowly and finely in the morality play of life.

CHAPTER 9

Spiritual Darkness

Despite our spiritual nature, there are many people who live in spiritual darkness. Despite the veneer of civility, many individuals are cauldrons of hostility, resentment and jealousy. Due to personal failings of their own, their goal is the diminution of others. They may resent your open spirit and friendliness. Some people at work and in your daily life act as if there is no judgment and that they are immune from the consequences of their behavior. They leave home in the morning smug in the thought that their fraudulent, or malicious behavior, will not be found out.

Some individuals are also what I call "predators". They are self-serving, quick to use or injure others, and to discredit them out of pettiness, spite or envy for their personal gain. They lack empathy and do not feel the pain of others. Their spirit is dormant and their souls lie fallow. Some are so morose, or sullen, in their spirits that they cannot respond to friendship or gracious treatment. When an opportunity presents itself, they will return your friendship with betrayal. They are often emotionally unbalanced and cannot quench the fire in their spirit. Their evil acts are a reflection of the hatred in their hearts. The smallest of their deeds, however, are observed and transparent to the spirit world and to others around them. Through their actions, they tempt fate and bring hardship and bad luck to themselves.

Besides the gratuitous behavior of mean spirited people, there are also sociopaths, psychopaths, paranoid and narcissist individuals in our society. Some of them may be on medication to help control their behavior. Some of them may insult, distort information, lie and malign you for their personal objectives and goals. They can be surreptitious in their behavior. If you resist, or defend yourself, it may only increase their negative behavior and in some cases increase "the fires of hatred in their brain". If you are faced by a person who is acting strangely or disproportionality in their responses to you, become alert to the possible reason and avoid them. If you are a victim, when possible, return an adverse act in a suitable manner or with a word of caution to others. There is accountability for all evil and sinful deeds. You are also instruments of atonement. The perpetrators must understand the consequences of their actions, in order for them to stop. Do not get angry. Back away if possible, you cannot reason with them. One can only hope that they will not cross your path.

Lost souls only deceive and diminish themselves. Despite their guile, self-satisfaction and feelings of invincibility, they will suffer in their lives and spirits far more than the suffering that they may inflict upon others. They incur a heavy debt on their souls. What they think is a solid foundation in their lives is "shifting sand". Their lives will be fragile and can become unraveled at any moment. Anything can happen at any time, whether in health, position or family, and will be to their immediate or future loss. They shall be deemed among the lost and shall atone in "spiritual darkness". Their atonement and retribution are sure and ordained. Life is full of pitfalls and potential misfortunes which they will unwittingly invite upon themselves. The consequences of their actions will eventually become clear to them. Your negative thoughts alone will bear upon them. The collective negative thoughts of many people will affect them. Your benign neglect and quiet amusement will confound them. In view of any damage to your good name, spirit and fortune that they may have caused, your forgiveness will be one of the hardest virtues. Your forbearance and forgiveness, however, will be a blessing for you.

Sinful and evil persons only deceive and diminish themselves.

People who do not live in harmony and love with others will face two consequences. The first is that every negative or positive thing that they do to another person, they are also doing it to themselves. Second, their actions will shape their character and the future events that will befall them. Their sins will "cling" to them and remain in the memory of others. Eventually, after they pass over, they will judge themselves and feel the pain that they have caused others. People like to say, "What goes around comes around". Indeed, this observation is true. Sooner or later the consequences of their actions will rebound upon them. It will not be intended to serve as a punishment but as a means to teach them empathy and how it feels to be hurt or cheated in the same way.

What you are doing to others, you are doing to yourself.

Fortunately, you will be protected from the behavior of malicious people by the many good people who will come to your help and defense. Many such people will know you by your reputation. They will recognize your value and come "out of the woodwork" when needed! They reflect the virtue of the human spirit and love. Pick your friends and associates carefully. Avoid unsavory people with animosity. Such people will frustrate your better nature and create stress in your life. They will test your better nature and indeed are envious of it. They could frustrate, or detour, your plans despite your best intentions.

Everyone is tested by their personal trials and misfortunes. Resist your lesser self. Do not diminish your spirit. Those of you who strive to increase your spiritual worth are free of harm. Endeavor to maintain the serenity in your lives. Avoid vexations, unnecessary conflicts and bad feelings toward others. When someone does a good deed for you, double and return their gesture.

Double and return every good deed that you receive.

CHAPTER 10

Religion

The Religious Instinct

From the beginning of time, many individuals have sensed their inner spirit. Religious sites have been found in Turkey that pre-dates the pyramids by several centuries. They are stone monuments of much larger scale and complexity than Stonehenge in England. There were no homes or signs of settlements in their vicinity. Apparently, the hunter and gatherers of the period only congregated there for some type of worship. Archeologists believe that these early people were drawn by a religious instinct. It is also estimated that settlements and agriculture followed and occurred after these religious sites, rather than before them. These early spiritual feelings led to the formation of the multiple faiths that we have today. Faith and spiritual yearning led to our houses of worship. Their message is the same, although their practices and dogmas may differ. The expression of faith led to the arts and music. Our religious instinct binds us in love and family. Thanks to our free choice, we stumble along the way.

Many attempts have been made to describe God. We cannot describe God. We can only know him by seeing a mother's love for her child, in a baby's smile and in our art and creations. We can only know him though our spiritual feelings, instincts and love for each other. We can only know him by listening to our inner voice, and the sound of the wind, song, and music. In effect, if we only paid attention, it may only be possible to know God through our "consciousness of God". One can only speculate that God is the power and energy of the cosmos. He is an organizing and unifying force that gives structure and order to the universe at each level of organization down to its lowest level. His living and eternal spirit empowers the universe and all living things upon it.

We can only know God through our "consciousness of God".

Organized Religion

The religion that we adopt, usually by the accident of birth, is the accepted vehicle for the expression of our faith. The religious or spiritual instinct is universal, and reaches out and is manifested in all of us despite our designated religion. Each religion is an important outlet for the spiritual yearnings of its adherents. Each religion has men and women of good faith, who follow the basic principles of their religion such as love, faith and goodwill. There are many fine religious leaders in all faiths who speak in God's name. They waken the spirit in our hearts and help us in our spiritual development, and comfort us in time of need. They help us grieve and support the important periods and transitions of our life, such as birth, marriage, or the death of a loved one. All religious organizations and their clergy are a blessing. They serve as God's shepherds. We know them by their open and sweet spirit and the temperance of their words.

The religious or spiritual instinct is universal. It reaches out and is manifested in all of us. Some members of the clergy like to find and promote miracles, as a way of demonstrating God's existence. They do not realize that life and the spirit that resides in us is the miracle. Our thoughts, hearing and vision that spring from our flesh are the miracle, not some apparition or "vision". We do not need "magic, miracle, and mystery" to prove God's existence. We are the result and proof of his existence.

All religious organizations and their clergy are a blessing.

All scripture originated from the same or similar inspirations. They are essentially symbolic, have multiple meanings, and in some cases cannot be interpreted literally. The spirit of revelation continues today and will in the future. As each new religion was introduced, many rushed in to gain ownership with their own interpretation. Unfortunately, religions have been distorted by such zealots who have imposed their own views. Many religious dogmas have also been created that are harmful and unnecessary for our spiritual growth.

Too many people have forgotten the commonality of our religious instinct and faith and have let it be hijacked by the self-serving. Some religious leaders like to proclaim that their religion is superior to the other religions. But, how does one measure the depth of one's devotion and faith expressed in any religion? Can we determine which religion has the most faithful adherents? Such persons are examples of a "true believer." It is not a question of faith but dogma that they adhere to. They are so invested in their doctrine that they fail to understand the basic purpose and true meaning of religion. Their rigidity of thought is devoid of faith and brotherhood. Forbearance is also forgotten when religious leaders, and some of their followers, make gratuitous attacks against another religion. The denigration of other religions does not enhance the truth of their religion. Their words lead to intolerance and conflict. Such leaders do not understand the enormity of their distortions and misdeeds. Some religious groups also assume an attitude of arrogance and lack of responsibility for other groups outside their faith.

In all religions, the strident, sick and distorted spirit uses their religion as an emotional outlet for the domination and attack on others. They take portions of the religious texts out of context, and use them to distort the message of their own and other religions. They justify and rationalize their attacks in the name of God. They use God's name in vain with their distorted dogmas and beliefs. It matters not which religion they presume to speak for. They are not men of faith. They poison relationships with other religions and groups. Goodwill suffers in their presence. Beware of these so called religious people or "false prophets" who preach words without understanding, and spread malicious dogma for their own needs, self-importance and your domination. The misunderstanding, as well as animosity, between religions can be laid at the feet of these religious zealots.

Religion should also stay out of government. A theological state can and does lead to abuses. Some secular and theocratic governments use religion as a means to promote their policies and power. Religion should only enhance the individual spirit, rather than the governance of religious laws. Only faith, love, tolerance and goodwill should be their message. Unless they are teachers, those who claim to know God's word should keep it to themselves and not impose their interpretations and dogmas on others. Religion is a personal matter. There is no personal salvation or gain by the domination of others, or the imposition of religious laws.

> *Only faith, love and goodwill should be the message of religious leaders.*

Persons of Faith

The important question is not the religion we have adopted, but are we persons of faith and goodwill? Such individuals dignify their religion, rather than their religion adding dignity to them. Regardless of religious affiliation, all faith is the same and all good men of faith are the same. Many different faiths and paths lead to God. No path is superior to the other. Only the development of our spirit and moral worth is important, regardless of the path taken. The religious impulses that make us a Christian, Jew, Moslem, or any other faith, are the same. All such men of faith recognize each other. In this regard, we are brothers and should respect each other as brothers. The Christians believe that God had a son. This belief does not exclude others from their own spiritual divinity. We are all God's sons and daughters.

Our instinct and belief in God is universal. We must not forget the commonality of our faith and let it be hijacked by others. The three great monotheistic religions must once again find their shared faith and values and treat each other with respect. Persons of faith whether clergy or lay, must speak up and stop the targeted slander of each other's faith by the misguided among us. Value your religion. It is the source of your faith and belief in a higher power. Whatever religion it may be, it is the spiritual path to your creator. The important thing to remember is that all men of faith, regardless of their specific religious belief, are the same in their heart.

All persons of faith are the same in their heart.

Today the spirit can be overwhelmed and drowned out by the incessant drum beat of the media and its rush to the lowest common denominator. The rules of decorum, polite conversation and courtship are lost. Sex and indecency are exploited by the media. In such an environment, many lose their way. You must not succumb. Listen to that small voice of your spirit that will not be extinguished. Resist temptation and do not commit moral suicide. Love, decency, and virtue are real. They are part of your spiritual being.

Love, decency and virtue are real.

A Good Person

A person of faith is also a good person. A good person is the epitome of goodwill. They are known by their respectful treatment of others. They do not intentionally hurt anyone with a harsh word or rudeness. They do not exploit, or use, anyone for their personal gain. They are considerate, loyal and greet others with goodwill. They help the less fortunate and help others grow and prosper. They honor their contracts and keep their word, and do not abuse their position or authority. They give each person their due, and do not cater to garner favor. Their heart harbors no animosity. They come to the support of others when injustice is done, and defend them against injustice. They visit the sick and give words of encouragement to the despondent. They do not judge others. They injure no one in word or deed.

They have a fierce moral clarity. Their goodwill and personal dignity is obtained through their habituation of virtue. They do not compromise their standards to please others. They challenge the malicious gossip of others, and do not take part in less than honorable deeds. They are known by their personal behavior and the indivisibility of their integrity. They are modest, neither loud nor brash, without excessive display of wealth or position. They are not haughty, prideful or vainglorious. They are patient in adversity and do not complain in hardship. They exhibit a quiet moral courage. They can be recognized by their modesty, perseverance in hardship, their discipline under stress, their courage to take risks, to do their duty and to take care of their families. They are also candid, sincere, know who they are and have quiet self-esteem.

A good person has a fierce moral clarity.

They add value to your life and enrich your experiences. They are generous in their charity. They help those in need when not asked, speak well of others who have been maligned, and support the advancement of their friends and colleagues. They are a dissenting voice against injustice. A good person is gracious and shows gratitude for small courtesies. They help soften the hearts of strangers, in another wise ungracious and uncaring world. Good persons are found at every level of educational achievement, income level, position and social standing. Many "respected' persons in society fall short of these criteria.

A good person is a dissecting voice against injustice.

A good person is the quiet basis of peace and prosperity and is the moral counterweight to those who use and abuse the world and its people for their own gain. A good person helps to stabilize the world and assure its orderly functioning. The integrity of a good person is the foundation of commerce and contributes to the safety of society. You only have to look at peaceful societies and those that are torn asunder, to understand what occurs when there is a deficit of good people.

The influence of a good person is beyond calculation. Whether they live in a humble home or in a mansion, they have a great impact on the world. They, unknowingly, influence the spirits and well-being of people far and near. Their words of encouragement, or good deeds, are repeated by those they have touched. They reinforce and support others with their smiles, love and warmth. They serve as a model for others. Like stone hitting water, their impact ripples endlessly as those they have influenced support and sustain others. Because of their sweet and unassuming spirit they are unaware of their influence, and wonder what they may have contributed to the world. Their ultimate success in life is not having hurt any person by word, deed or act. They do not owe any person an apology for wrong doing or injury. Their life's success is a pure and unencumbered spirit.

> *The deeds of a good person ripple outwards, like stone hitting water.*

By contrast, the arrogance of the rude and self-serving person hangs like a "cloud" over those they associate with. Their presence is an offense to many. They are a plague to themselves and others. They find no joy or contentment in their possessions and live with a contentious heart. Their spirits are hollow and vacuous. Many display wealth or use their position to enhance their self-importance. However, they have diminished stature among people and receive no respect from them.

> *A good person has an indivisible integrity.*

CHAPTER 11

Age and Death

Age

If you feel that you are only flesh and a victim of age, so shall it be. Your body will deteriorate in accordance with your beliefs about old age, due to the power of suggestion. Many people age themselves unnecessarily and prematurely. They age by abusing the beautiful body that they were born with. They age because of drugs, excessive alcohol and tobacco. They age because of over indulgence in their diet and lack of exercise. These behaviors can be considered a sin against themselves, since they reduce the quality of their life and shorten their spiritual development. Their physical age is further affected by their attitudes, perceptions and expectations about age. They age because they think they are supposed to age. They age by watching and emulating others as they age. They age by adopting an "image" of old age. They age in the same manner that you pick up local accents and by adopting local expectations and perceptions. Some people unconsciously model themselves after the older people that they see or associate with in their area. Do not assume an attitude of defeat and hopelessness and wait for your demise, as some older people do. Do not enter assisted living or nursing homes unless absolutely necessary. It is a voluntary acceptance of your demise and will accelerate it. You will unconsciously adopt the characteristics of and become like the people that you see around you.

Your time on earth is finite. Do not squander it. What you may lose in your physical decline, you gain in wisdom, insight and maturity.

As you age, do not despair that your life is almost over. Your spirit is ever expanding with new adventures to come. Do not fear your demise. Do not accept the concept of decay and death. Your future is still young with opportunity. While earlier goals may have been met, make new plans and strive toward them. You are younger than you think and your potential for growth remains. By planning, your plans will pull you into the future. Not to continue planning and striving as you grow older, will only hasten your decline. As you mature, do not stop your plans or dreams.

Your plans will pull you into the future.

While your body ages, your spirit grows. Your spirit is ageless and forever young. It changes and grows in its moral worth, as you progress on your spiritual journey. Only your physical body gets older. You feel only the spirit within you and not your physical age. Love also never ages and is forever. Your older age is not the end, but at the threshold of a new beginning. Ultimately, your true age is your attitude toward age. Grow older with grace and maturity and live your life to the fullest to the last moment. Do not dwell on sickness and nurse your illnesses. Those fortunate to have grown with spiritual beauty, retain that beauty and age with grace. Some individuals fail to grow in spiritual worth. They fail to become a warm and loving "human being" despite their age. They continue and persist in their angry and unhappy ways. It reflects in their appearance and behavior.

Your spirit is ageless and eternally young.

Maintain a youthful anticipation of your next life on the other side. Just as you look forward to any trip, have the same anticipation for your new home to come. At that time, if you bring experiences full of evil deeds, such as deceit and harm to others, you will dwell in remorse. If your experiences are full of beauty, happiness and good deeds, you will dwell in happiness.

Death

In death, you will fold back into God's love. Those with spiritual value, and who age with grace, will pass over with grace. Those who have lived in spiritual darkness, and do not age with grace, will pass over with resistance and hardship. When you pass over, you will fly to God as a bird flies to its nest. As birth is the morning of a new day, death is only the evening. It is your spirit that sheds its body, not your body that gives up its spirit! Only your body is lost. Your consciousness continues. You will live in a spiritual reality rather than a physical reality. Death is merely a change of form whereby your consciousness departs and continues without your body. Your consciousness continues in God's larger consciousness and presence. Your death is the price of birth and is only part of another cycle to consolidate your worldly experiences.

> *When you pass over, you will fly to God as a bird flies to its nest.*

Do not fear death, but only fear the person you are at the time of death. All souls will come to God bare and exposed. In many instances, you may unconsciously choose the time of your death. Your death may occur when your immediate spiritual mission has been fulfilled. It may occur when your spiritual growth has reached a temporary stopping point and needs consolidation. It may occur when you wish to join your loved ones who have gone on before you. You may also die young, as atonement for actions in your present or former life.

> *Do not fear death, but only fear the person you are at the time of death.*

Only your body that has belonged to the earth has returned to it. Your graveyards are places of deception. Your graveyards support the illusion of those who believe that there is only one life. Treat the grave site only as a memorial to your loved one's living and eternal spirit. What lies there, belongs only to the earth. Their spirit and reality is with God. Go to the resting place of their remains only to help bring their memory and spirit closer to you. To consider them dead is to deny their living spirit. As we have lived in God's spirit, he has lived through us. As we have loved him, he has loved us. Having loved us, would he abandon us in death? We are always in his presence and are eternal. Strive to die rich in good deeds, memories and love.

> *They are only dead who are dead in spirit.*

CHAPTER 12

The Hereafter

Heaven

After you pass over, you will meet your loved ones who have gone on before. They wait for you and know when you have passed over. Parents will rush to meet their children. A parent's excitement is a joy to behold as they greet their children. Your friends will once again embrace you. You will be reunited in friendship and love. You will revive former social relationships and rejoice in the love and friends around you. This will be your heaven, the heaven that you have created with the deeds and spiritual growth of your life on earth. Those with good deeds shall dwell in bliss, and feel the thoughts of their love ones who are still living. The positive feelings and attitudes about your memory will reach you and add to your happiness in God's presence.

In heaven parents will rush to greet their children.

The degree of your spiritual adjustment will be relative to the state of your spirit at the time of passing. If you were a person of faith, and a good person, you will find bliss, happiness and love. If you have denied God, you will dwell in confusion. You will review your experiences on earth. You will assess whether your spiritual goals have been met or if you caused pain to others. Your spiritual state and continued growth will depend upon its level of development and moral worth at the time of your death. You will judge yourself. Those who have proven themselves, and have added to their spiritual value, will continue their spiritual growth. If you have committed evil, you will reside in spiritual darkness. In heaven, you will view your earthly life as a dream. You will continue to resolve issues and consolidate the experiences of your past and former lives.

You will judge yourself.

There will be no deception or false pride. Those who have inflicted harm will dwell in the memory of their deeds. They will repent of them until that time they can return to earth to make amends. Those who bring an open and wholesome heart will rejoice and continue their spiritual growth in their new home. The richest and most powerful will be equal to the simplest man. He who returns with a pure and open heart shall be honored. The richest and most powerful of men with shameful deeds will be considered among the lowest. A person's celebrity status on earth, depending on how it was earned, can become a badge of shame. You will judge whether you left the world a better place than you found it? Did you help your fellow man, when his need was obvious and without being asked? Did you add to the paradise that was created for you? Did you leave without debt or harm to any one?

Hell

Those who have sinned excessively, and committed evil deeds, will find themselves in a state of "hell." There is no physical place of hell. They will be in a spiritual state of what they perceive as "hell", relative to the degree of their deeds and moral worth. It will begin at the moment of their passing, when they will sense that there is no one to grieve for them. The negative thoughts, of those still living and who have passed over, will reach them and leave them no peace until their atonement.

Hell is a dark night of remorse.

Those who have committed evil acts, and the worst among us, will go into a nightmare like slumber of tortured thoughts. It will be their "dark night." They will experience a "nightmare" reviewing their sins on earth as in a bad dream. They will feel and experience the pain that they have caused others. Their feelings and emotions will consist of guilt, remorse, regret and shame. It will be a place of darkness, disturbing dreams and thoughts devoid of love. Their spiritual darkness will continue until they are remorseful for their behavior and are ready to return to life on earth to atone for their former deeds.

> *You will feel and experience the pain that you have caused others.*

Reincarnation

It may take several life times to develop your spirit and atone for your sins. You will return to earth to face new challenges, to continue your growth in moral worth, and atone for previous sins. If someone was a murderer, he may be murdered to experience and feel the loss of his former victim. If he was cruel and violent, he may be exposed to similar situations. A person's opportunities and experiences may also be kept within certain boundaries, relative to their previous behavior on earth. A previously vain glorious person may have their success limited to a preordained level. Persons with deep and abiding love in a past life may also meet again. The spirits of unborn children may also pick their parents, to continue a past loving relationship, or to work out problems of a previous life time. They may also seek a special environment to continue their spiritual growth.

> *Children pick their parents.*

Like nature you have your seasons and cycles. You will be reborn as sure as the sun rises each morning. You will return like the leaves in the Spring, as sure as Spring follows Winter. As a tree becomes dormant and grows in strength after each Winter season, so will your spiritual strength mature. Each rebirth renews and refreshes the world with new energy and with former mental boundaries and constraints erased. The signs of rebirth are all around you.

> *You will be reborn as sure as Spring follows Winter.*

You will come back to earth as a more refined and mature person. As your body limits your consciousness to here and how, it will block the memory of your previous life times. As a flower returns from the seed or a bulb, it is not the same identical flower but it springs from its original source. In a similar manner, your re-birth is a new beginning and fresh challenge for you without the burden of false beliefs and old regrets. You will not return as a blank page. You will continue your spiritual development at a more advanced stage and help others in their growth. Some may still continue to suffer, in order to complete their atonement, or to fully assure their repentance and empathy. Your spiritual growth and development will continue as other facets of your eternal spirit are challenged. Your new life will either blossom or face severe challenges, depending upon your moral worth or debt. You will recycle on earth until you become worthy of remaining with God in love forever in eternity. With your spiritual perfection, there will no longer be any need for reincarnation. Indeed, you may become an emissary and angel of God.

The sophistication and emotional maturity of some people are a carryover of their previous lives and development. Notice the sociability and personality of small children. It could not be developed in their short lives. It is the result and testament of their earlier sojourn on earth which has been brought forward. Some of you have spirits older than others and are more oriented to the welfare of your fellow man. Some, whose lives had been cut off early, will return to visit loved ones, or children who they had not had a chance to know in their previous life. The thoughts and prayers of their loved ones will also help to bring them back.

> *The sweetness and maturity of small children is a testament to their previous live times.*

CHAPTER 13

Conclusion

We are conscious and spiritual projections of God's spirit that is living a mortal life. God's reality creates us, flows through us and sustains us at every moment. In view of our free will and choice, we are challenged to grow in moral value and spiritual worth. Our living and eternal spirit is affected by every action in our life. Our moral worth, and assured atonement for our negative deeds, explains every aspect and occurrence in our life. Our goal is to develop our eternal soul and become closer to God in love.

We are conscious and spiritual projections of God's spirit.

Rejoice in your creation as part of God's spirit. Embrace the journey that you have been embarked upon. Accept your spiritual challenge. You are here for a reason. You are responsible for your own behavior. To remain morally passive, in view of your challenges and opportunities, is a denial of your spirit. Be alert to your spiritual needs and atone for your misdeeds. To be passive in life and unaware of your spiritual responsibility will lead to your being buffeted by random forces beyond your control. The consequences of an ignored spirit are failure, unhappiness and an unfulfilled life.

Rejoice in your creation as part of God's spirit.

Those who do not recognize and accept God's existence have a veil over their eyes. They will live vainglorious lives without understanding and meaning. Resist any influence that can limit or distort your personal development, spiritual growth, and happiness. Fight any injustice to yourself and others as a responsibility to your spiritual self. Resist perfidy of any kind. You will be held accountable for your actions and inactions. Love, decency and virtue are real. Your spiritual goal is love and avoidance of injury to any person in word or deed.

Love, virtue and decency are real.

Live with love, grace and goodwill. What you are doing to others, you are doing to yourself. Every action, or inaction of your life, reflects your spiritual value. Your attention, or lack of attention to your moral worth, will facilitate or hinder the quality of your life in this world and the next. Unless you face your moral responsibilities and develop your spiritual worth, you will forfeit your virtue and honor. Those who fail to develop their better selves will endure their worst characteristics.

As you become aware of your spiritual nature and develop it, your lives will flourish and become happier and content. You will be blessed with serenity. Your stress will be less and your body's health will be enhanced. You will be protected from life's greater misfortunes. You will age gracefully, without fear of death. As the sun rises each morning, refresh your living and eternal spirit with faith, love and goodwill. Those of us who have completed their journey, and have achieved perfection, will reside in his presence for eternity. They are perfect souls. They too watch over us and intercede for us.

Your character is your destiny.

APPENDIX A

Racial and National Diversity

Racial Diversity

Why are there different races? It is part of God's creativity expressed through the diversity of people and races. It is a challenge and test of our spiritual development and tolerance of racial differences. Like flowers, the different colors in man approach the spectrum of the rainbow, so that we can recognize and be different from each other. Diversity among people challenges our personal growth through interaction with one another and tolerance of our differences. Each race excels in some characteristics, but shares in them all. Together, we are a garden of diversity and capabilities. Through our differences and interactions, we accelerate each other's development and gain from each other's practices and culture.

The sum of all races is a perfect whole.

One race or culture is not superior to another in terms of spiritual value and quality of life. Some industrial nations think that they are superior because of their material development. They may think that they have a right to exploit or dominate others. One cannot assume that one culture is superior to another. It is the development of the spirit that is important, not the acquisition of material possessions. Some races may appear culturally and materially inferior to you, yet their spiritual worth is equal to any other, and they face the same spiritual challenges. The humanity of man is a constant, regardless of culture, and can be found in the most remote corner of the world. The richest nations can have a poverty of spirit.

> *The humanity of man is a constant, regardless of race or culture.*

National Diversity

As the personalities of people differ, so do the personal characteristics of people of different nations differ. The variation of personalities between nations also represents different parts of a perfect whole. Nations interact and balance each other much like the interactions of individual people. They are a part of a larger plan to create checks and balances between the agendas of different nations and their national characteristics. Similar national groups are prone to conflict, due to the rejection of what they see of themselves in the other. This in part explains the persecution of similar groups by each other, as witnessed in recent history in Europe and the Middle East. Such nations are closer in their characteristics, than they realize.

Strife due to racial, religious or cultural differences is also due to less developed souls who hate themselves. Individuals of some nations think that they are superior to others and that, unlike themselves, they are less human and less important. Such people pay a price for their attitudes and behavior through eventual defeat or other calamity. All nations must tolerate and respect their differences and not subjugate those they think are of lesser stature.

> *Strife due to racial, religious or cultural differences is due to less developed souls who hate themselves.*

The diverse national origins, capabilities and contributions of its citizens explain the success of America. As a new nation, it lacked the restrictive attitudes and practices of older societies, which unleased its potential. Older constraints and boundaries were removed. The best characteristics of each constituent national group were enhanced. This occurred through the checks and balances between national groups and the freedoms of democracy. People's beliefs and attitudes became open to new concepts and opportunities. The best characteristics and energies of diverse nationalities have created a dynamic national synergism. Because of this, America has been distinguished by the fairness and charity with which it has treated other nations. The allegiance of Americans to their former homelands has also contributed to this.

> *The personalities of different nations represent different parts of a perfect whole.*

A nation, as represented by the collective actions of its people, is also accountable for its actions. Unfortunately, some nations may lose their fairness and evenhandedness and support an aggressor nation in some regional conflicts. As a result, it too may experience problems. The ultimate fate of a nation will be found in the way it treats its neighbor and other nations. Good neighbor relations lead to mutual prosperity and growth. Dominance and the acquisition of a neighbor's land leads to hatred and loss for all parties involved. National and racial diversity was introduced to teach moderation and tolerance, and to enrich the fabric of our lives. The drama and challenge of spiritual growth continues as part of the dealings between national groups and races.

APPENDIX B

The Impact of Political Philosophies

Political ideologies, as well as religious extremism, have delayed or destroyed the personal and spiritual development of countless people, and have led to untold human misery and grief. Fascism under Hitler led to the death of millions and the destruction of civilization in Europe. Communism under Stalin and in China led to the shackling of millions, hunger and despair. The Pol Pot of Cambodia destroyed a beautiful serene country and wonderful people. Why, because of the ideologies of a few who gained control. Human growth can only prosper where personal freedom is available and where checks and balances exist to control the ideologies of those in power. Your spirit develops best in a free society. Your freedom like your spirituality comes from God.

> *Freedom of human initiative and enterprise assure prosperity and spiritual growth.*

Democracy

Democracy provides the environment and opportunity to assure individual development and prosperity. Freedom of human initiative and enterprise are protected by the "checks and balances" of a democratic government that controls the greed of men. Democracy provides the environment for the competition of ideas, competing truths and personal development. It is vital for the release of human capabilities and spirit. Protect your democracy. Those who have lived under tyranny understand its critical importance.

Do not take your freedom and liberty for granted. If you do not protect your freedom, you will lose it. Without checks and balances, the lesser among you can gain power and impose their tyranny upon you. The success of democracy depends upon leaders with competence, integrity and good character. Freedom and prosperity depend upon a high level of moral worth and religious foundation, in the majority of its citizens. It is they who hold the fabric of your nation together, assure its functioning, and the election of qualified leaders. Democracy also depends upon an honest system of enforcement and integrity in its judicial system. An unbiased and free press is also essential. Democracy and economic freedom are essential for your personal and spiritual development.

> *The success of democracy depends upon leaders and citizens with competence and moral value.*

Beware of immoral and corrupt politicians. Their goal is power and domination and not your well-being. They assume that their needs and values are superior to yours. Resist those who would squander the resources of your earth without care or regulation. Mind control, or any control of the freedom of thought or of the press, must not be tolerated. Do not let anyone tell you how to live. There are too many who are sufficiently insecure in their economic, social or religious dogmas that they seek to impose them on others. Do not be passive in your societies. Express your doubts and be outraged by the excesses of others that destroy your common home. Vote when you can. The will of the collective society can impose change and influence the will of its leaders. Do not lose the power of the vote that you have in a democracy.

> *Resist those who through their dogmas block the human spirit and the development of its potential.*

Socialism

Be alert to the "potential pitfalls" of socialism. Socialists' profess a value system in helping the poor and less fortunate, without charity at a personal level. They find their morality in public policy issues. They need to control how others live and think in order to compensate for their own insecurity. Radical socialists consider truth and integrity an impediment to achieving their goals. They will resort to any deception to achieve them. It is on a continuum to the right of communism. It can quickly shift to the left, depending upon the existing social or political climate and political opportunity.

A socialist does not want self-reliance and initiative on your part. If their policies are adopted, it reassures their insecurities and doubts. It demonstrates to themselves and others that they are caring people. Their lives achieve structure and security by imposing their radical socialist agendas and dogmas on others. They thrive on a dependent rather than a self-reliant society. They attempt to level society and distribute wealth. They have contempt for and constrain the entrepreneur and job creator, but love the worker. As a result, jobs are lost and workers are impoverished. Their welfare state creates economic and spiritual poverty. To counter opposing views, they will limit or try to impede the freedom of speech. When in power, they will restrict or chip away at your freedom and economic opportunities. Today's Liberal/Progressive activists in the media do not realize that they are mindlessly undermining the foundations of their own success and of their children. They are dismantling the checks and balances of our Constitution. While they participate and can flourish in a democratic society, they undermine it when given the opportunity.

Socialists need the security and structure of their dogma.

Communism

Beware of communism, and other authoritarian governments, that suppress freedom and religion. They neither admit, nor recognize, a higher power than themselves. The worst characteristics of human beings flourish due to total control and a lack of checks and balances. Karl Marx, despite his "noble" but naive vision, did not understand this. The intolerance and control that they impose in the name of social good destroys human resolve, personal initiative, and impoverishes everyone. Communists naively think that they know better than you and that they can organize and dictate your life. Their total power is intoxicating to them. Their proposed aims may be "noble", but their results are disastrous. Religion and spiritual activities are forbidden and suppressed in the name of their higher power. Millions of people in China, Russia, East Germany and former Eastern bloc countries and Cambodia have been murdered as dissenters and threats to their power.

Prosperity cannot be achieved on the backs of others.

Governmental control by religious groups should also be avoided. Those who presume to speak for God are also anxious to impose their dogmas and narrow beliefs. You must use your own judgment and ability to reason. Be vigilant and protect your spiritual heritage as a free person. Beware of dogmas and the self-righteous. A river of tears has flowed, due to the cruelty of tyrannical governments. Resist those that block the human spirit and the development of its potential. Unless you resist tyranny, political or religious, you will suffer and may die under their oppression.

War

Nations, which cannot live with each other, attack each other. The spiritual poverty of its leaders, embroil its people for national gain or power. Too often, and unfortunately, their policies are embraced by their people. War is abhorred by those who treasure peace. However, those who do not defend their home when unjustly attacked will lose it. War brings out the worst and best in mankind. Unfortunately, it emboldens the worst persons to do evil deeds, and unleashes the sociopath and psychopath personality among its soldiers.

War also brings out the best behavior in those of good character, to protect their homes and nation. For them, it is a time of honor, duty, sacrifice and brotherhood. In earlier times, battle was a way to develop character and discipline. The good person does their duty and shows bravery. For this reason, they are usually the first to die. They test their mettle and are found to be worthy. The individual and group challenges imposed by war lead to comradeship. Due to the sacrifices that people and soldiers make for each other, more love is born in war than in peaceful times.

More love is born in war than in peace.

Too many young men have been sacrificed in the prime of their lives for questionable goals. However, no soldier who dies in defense of his country dies in vain. Although unfortunate, those who die in war are only "fallen". Their valor is not lost. They dwell among their comrades. They have honored themselves with their courage and call to duty. Their spirits exists and are honored in God's presence. When they again return to earth, they will prosper in all of the blessings that they had freely forfeited in their young lives. They will meet their loved ones again. As society matures, the world is progressing and slowly becoming a more harmonious place. Despite the continuing carnage in the world, it is getting less as the spiritual value of its inhabitant's continue to develop and increase over the centuries.

REFERENCES

Armstrong, Karen (1994). *A History of God: The 4000 Year - Quest of Judaism, Christianity and Islam*. Ballantine Books. New York.

Atwater, P.M.H. (2011). *Near Death Experiences*. MJF Books. New York.

Barker, Elsa. (1914). *Letters From A Living Dead Man*. E F Dutton and Company. New York.

Becker, E. (1973). *Denial of Death*. New York: Free Press.

Campbell, J. (1949). *The Hero with a Thousand Faces*. Princeton: University Press.

Campbell, J. (1972). *Myths to Live By*. New York: Bantam Books.

Campbell, J. (1987). *The Power of Myth*. New York: Doubleday.

Hull, R.F.C. (1971). *The Collected Works of C.G. Jung*. Princeton University Press.

Jung, C.G. "Instinct and the Unconscious". The British Journal of Psychology. 1919.

Ozkaptan, H. (2007). *Life's Purpose, Development of Your Living and Eternal Spirit*. Lulu Publishing, North Carolina.

Ozkaptan, H. (2010). *Islam and the Koran, Described and Defended.* Lulu Publishing, North Carolina.

Ozkaptan, H. (2012). *Beyond Love, The Fulfillment of Love and Marriage.* Lulu Publishing, North Carolina.

Parnia, S. (2013). *Erasing Death.* New York. Harper One.

Roberts, J. (1986). *Dreams and the Projection of Consciousnesss.* Walpole, New Hampshire: Stillpoint Publishing.

Roberts, J. (1994). *The Nature of Personal Reality.* Novato, Calif.: New World Library.

Ravi Rawat, BBC Video "Near Death Experience– Concept of Soul Justified", Films for the Humanities and Science, Undated.

Smed A. Jouni, Out-of-Body Experience Studies, Monroe Institute.

www.ingramcontent.com/pod-product-compliance
Lightning Source LLC
Chambersburg PA
CBHW031413040426
42444CB00005B/540